MW00453634

# Theory of Music Workbook

## for Trinity College London written examinations

## Grade 3

by Naomi Yandell

Published by
Trinity College London

Registered Office:
89 Albert Embankment
London SE1 7TP  UK

T +44 (0)20 7820 6100
F +44 (0)20 7820 6161
E music@trinitycollege.co.uk
www.trinitycollege.co.uk

Registered in the UK
Company no. 02683033
Charity no. 1014792

Designer and editor: Natasha Witts
Music processed by New Notations London
Printed in England by Halstan, Amersham, Bucks

Sixth impression, December 2013

# Grade 3 Theory of Music Syllabus from 2007

| | | |
|---|---|---|
| Section 1 | General multiple choice – 10 questions | *(10 marks)* |
| Section 2 | Writing scales, arpeggios, broken chords | *(15 marks)* |
| Section 3 | Correcting mistakes | *(10 marks)* |
| Section 4 | Transposition | *(15 marks)* |
| Section 5 | 4-part chords for SATB | *(15 marks)* |
| Section 6 | Adding a bass line to a tune or vice versa | *(15 marks)* |
| Section 7 | Analysis – 10 questions | *(20 marks)* |

Questions and tasks may cover all matters specified in previous grades and also the following:

## Rhythm

1. Compound time (time signatures of $\frac{6}{8}$, $\frac{9}{8}$ and $\frac{12}{8}$)
2. Grouping semiquavers and semiquaver rests in simple and compound time
3. Dotted quavers and dotted quaver rests in simple and compound time
4. Rules for grouping note and rest values within $\frac{6}{8}$, $\frac{9}{8}$ and $\frac{12}{8}$ time signatures
5. Quaver triplets
6. Anacrusis
7. Ties using new note values

## Pitch

1. Naming and using notes in treble or bass clefs (to three leger lines above or below the stave)
2. Bb and D major keys (for all major keys for the grade: scales, key signatures, one-octave arpeggios, broken chords and tonic triads (root or first inversion)
3. G and B minor keys (for all minor keys for the grade: scales – natural (Aeolian mode) and harmonic and melodic, key signatures, one-octave arpeggios, broken chords and tonic triads (root or first inversion)
4. Second inversions of major and minor tonic triads of keys covered so far
5. Identifying the key of a piece in Bb or D major and G or B minor
6. 5th degree of the major/minor scale being known as the dominant or soh
7. Dominant triads for all keys covered so far
8. Major/minor dominant triad labelled:
    – as a chord symbol above the music (e.g. G in the key of C major or E in the key of A minor)
    – as a Roman numeral below the music (e.g. V in the key of C major or v in the key of A minor)
9. 7th degree of the major/minor scale being known as the leading note
10. Understanding the term 'chord progression'
11. Recognising a perfect cadence in the home key (major or minor)
12. Intervals (major/minor 6th, major/minor 7th above any tonic for the grade)
13. Writing tonic chords in root position in any key for the grade as well-balanced 4-part chords for SATB
14. Real and tonal sequences
15. Similar and contrary motion
16. Transposing a tune up or down an octave from treble clef to bass clef and vice versa
17. Ranges of violin, flute, cello, bassoon, as defined in the workbook
18. Knowing that violin and cello are string instruments, flute and bassoon are woodwind instruments

## Musical words and symbols

### Dynamic and articulation marks
*Marcato*, *semi-staccato* (and signs and abbreviations for these where appropriate)

### Tempo, expression marks and other words and signs
*Al*, *alla*, *a tempo*, *con*, *da Capo al Fine*, *dolce*, down-bow, *e*, *ed*, *leggiero*, *ma*, *marziale*, *meno*, *mosso*, *moto*, *non*, *più*, *poco*, *tranquillo*, *troppo*, up-bow, *vivo* (and signs and abbreviations for these where appropriate)

Every effort has been made to trace and acknowledge all copyright owners. If any right has been omitted or if any detail is incorrect, Trinity College London apologises and will rectify this in any subsequent reprints following notification.

# Introduction

## Using this workbook

The writing in the boxes ☐ tells you:

- About the music that you sing, or play on your instrument

- What you need to know to pass your Trinity College London Grade 3 Theory of Music examination. Topics from previous grades of the syllabus should also be known

## Doing the tasks

- Use a pencil with a sharp point and a fairly soft lead so that you can easily rub out what you have written if you need to

- Be careful to be accurate with musical notes and signs – this will make a difference to your marks because the examiner must be able to read what you have written

- Read through the boxes to make sure you understand how to do the tasks and ask for help if you need it

- The first task in each section has usually been done for you in purple to show you what to do

- Use the picture of the piano keyboard on page 63. It is there to help you, even if you do not play a keyboard instrument

- **Always try to play, sing or tap the music you write.** This is a very important part of learning, and will help you 'hear' what you write in your head. It will help you in the examination when you have to work in silence

## What comes next?

When you have finished this book try some sample papers. You can download them from www.trinitycollege.co.uk/theory. You will then be ready to ask your teacher to enter you for the Grade 3 Theory of Music examination.

# Acknowledgements

Trinity College London would like to acknowledge the invaluable contribution to the development of this music theory programme by music teachers, professors, examiners, language specialists and students from around the world. Their comments have usefully informed the final shape of the workbooks and examination papers, and are much appreciated.

# New notes for Grade 3 𝄞 and 𝄢

LEDGER LINES !!

Here, in purple, are the new treble clef note names you need to know for Grade 3. You know the others from Grades 1 and 2.

MIDDLE C

E F G A B C D E F G A B C D E F G A B C D E F

**Remember**

Key signature flats or sharps apply to every note with the same note name (whatever the register).

1 Name the circled notes in the following music:

Haydn

E

Mozart

Scarlatti

Johann Strauss II

Mozart

etc.

Here, in purple, are the new bass clef note names you need to know for Grade 3. You know the others from Grades 1 and 2.

G  A  B  C  D  E  F  G  A  B  C  D  E  F  G  A  B  C  D  E  F  G  A

**2** Name the circled notes in the following music:

Mussorgsky

D♭  ___  ___    ___  ___  ___

**Remember**

An accidental lasts until another one on exactly the same line or space cancels it, or until the next bar line.

J S Bach

___  ___    ___  ___

Beethoven

___  ___    ___  ___  ___

Mahler

___  ___  ___  ___

Vivaldi

___  ___  ___  ___

# Note values and rests

1. **Semiquavers:**

So far you have seen semiquavers beamed together in groups of four where the beat is a crotchet:

However, composers sometimes write: ♪ or ♫ or ♫

If they do this, they will also probably need to use a quaver or semiquaver rest. This is because notes and rests should be grouped in crotchet beats where the beat is a crotchet.

Here is a **semiquaver rest:** ⁊

Here are some examples. The coloured boxes show how the semiquavers fit into the crotchet beat groupings:

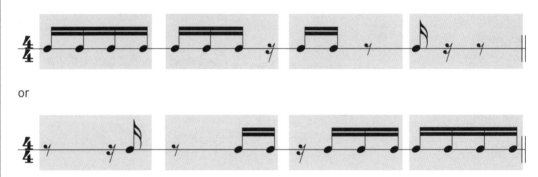

or

Do not use two semiquaver rests one after the other, except where each rest completes the crotchet beat:

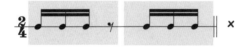

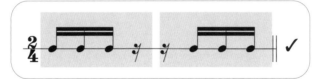

Sometimes rests are put inside crotchet beat groupings to make the music easier to read:

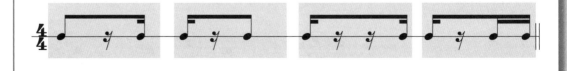

4

Handy tip!

Quavers and semiquavers are also often beamed together like this where the beat is a crotchet.

or

2. Here is a dotted quaver: ♪.

| Quaver (half a crotchet beat) ♪ | + | Single semiquaver (quarter of a crotchet beat) ♪ | = | Dotted quaver (three quarters of a crotchet beat) ♪. |

The dotted quaver is often followed by a single semiquaver because together they make up one crotchet beat:

More rarely the semiquaver comes first:

Here is a dotted quaver rest:

**1** Fill the coloured boxes with correctly grouped semiquavers.

**2** Write correctly grouped semiquavers below the asterisks (*).

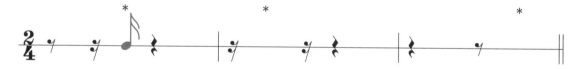

**3** Fill the coloured boxes with correctly grouped quaver or semiquaver rests.

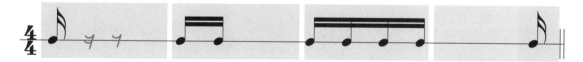

**4** Write correctly grouped quaver or semiquaver rests below the asterisks (*).

**5** The following music contains mistakes in the grouping of notes and rests. There are also some unnecessary ties. Write it out correctly.

Haydn

**6** Write 2-bar rhythms using quaver and semiquaver notes and rests. Include one dotted quaver note.

# Compound time signatures

So far all the time signatures you have learned are in **simple time**. They are called 'simple' because the beat in the bar (quaver, crotchet or minim) divides easily into **two** equal parts. For example, here are some simple time signatures with three beats in a bar:

**Handy tip!**
Here the coloured boxes help you to think in quaver, crotchet or minim groupings.

 (quaver beat easily divides into 2 semiquavers)

 (crotchet beat easily divides into 2 quavers)

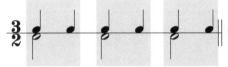 (minim beat easily divides into 2 crotchets)

This is not always the case. In some time signatures (known as **compound** time signatures) the beats in the bar divide easily into **three** equal parts.

For Grade 3 you need to know the following new time signatures; they all have a dotted crotchet as the main beat in the bar. Each dotted crotchet beat divides easily into three quavers:

**Handy tip!**
Here the coloured boxes help you to think in dotted crotchet beat groupings.

There is no number to show that the dotted crotchet is the type of beat to count so **8** is used and the quavers are grouped in threes for easy reading.

**1** Write the correct number of dotted crotchet beats in each of the following bars:

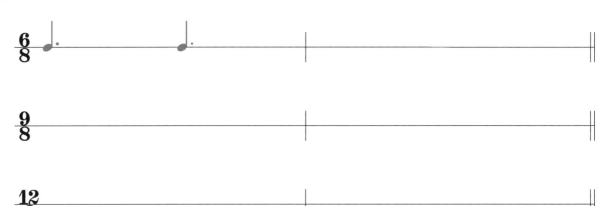

**2** Here is a mixture of simple and compound time signatures. Write the correct number of beats (quavers, crotchets, dotted crotchets or minims) in each of the following bars:

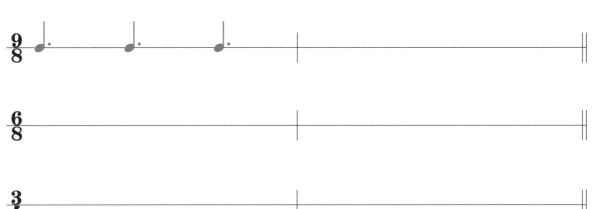

**3** Write the correct time signatures.

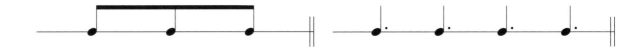

# Grouping notes in $\frac{6}{8}$, $\frac{9}{8}$ and $\frac{12}{8}$

**Handy tip!**

Here the coloured boxes help you to think in dotted crotchet beat groupings.

When grouping notes in $\frac{6}{8}$, $\frac{9}{8}$ and $\frac{12}{8}$ think in dotted crotchet beat groupings to make the music easy to read. Here are a few examples to show the difference between good and bad grouping:

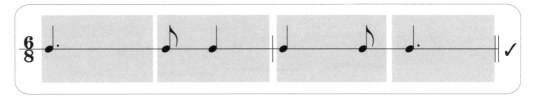

**Did you know?**

Ties should not be used within a dotted crotchet beat.

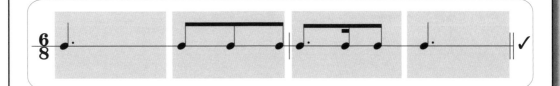

**Handy tip!**

Notes are also grouped together in dotted crotchet beat groupings in $\frac{3}{8}$ even though it is officially a simple time signature.

Where the main beat is a dotted crotchet, semiquavers are often beamed together in groups of six.

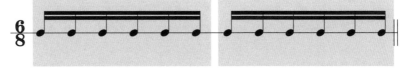

Where there are fewer than six semiquavers, they are beamed within the dotted crotchet groupings, for example:

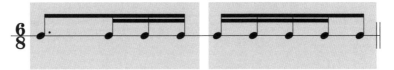

Notes taking up a whole bar should be written like this:

**1** Look at the following music. Add bar lines to agree with the time signatures.

Beethoven

Borodin

Foster

J S Bach

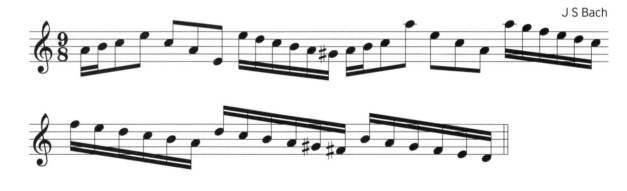

Traditional (African)

Schubert

**2** The following music contains mistakes in the grouping of notes. Write it out correctly.

D'Indy

Mendelssohn

Handel

Traditional (English)

**Handy tip!**

Here the coloured boxes help you to think in dotted crotchet beat groupings.

**Handy tip!**

Crotchet rests always come before quaver rests within a dotted crotchet beat.

When grouping rests in $\frac{6}{8}$, $\frac{9}{8}$ and $\frac{12}{8}$ think in dotted crotchet beat groupings. Here are a few examples to show you the difference between good and bad groupings.

1. Bars where there are dotted crotchet silences:

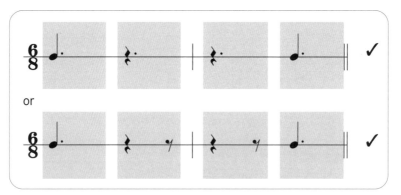

or

2. Bars where there are rests worth two dotted crotchet beats at the beginning of a bar:

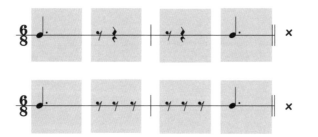

As you know, a whole bar of silence is always shown by a semibreve rest, whatever the time signature:

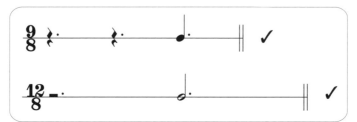

**1** Write correctly grouped rests below the asterisks (*).

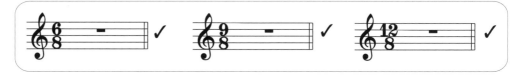

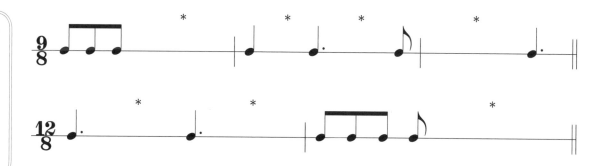

2 The following music contains mistakes in the grouping of rests. Write it out correctly.

J S Bach

Mozart

3 Look at the following music. Add bar lines to agree with the time signatures.

Holst

Anon

Beethoven

# Writing your own tunes to a given rhythm

**1** Write a tune for violin using the first five degrees of the scale of E minor to the given rhythm. Use a key signature and finish on the tonic.

## Handy tip!

See page 62 for the ranges of the violin and cello (string instruments) and the flute and bassoon (woodwind instruments).

**2** Write a tune for flute using the notes of the tonic triad in A minor to the given rhythm. Use a key signature and finish on the tonic.

**3** Write a tune for bassoon using the first five degrees of the scale of D minor to the given rhythm. Use a key signature and finish on the tonic.

## Did you know?

The violin and flute are known as **treble instruments** (their music uses the treble clef). The cello and bassoon are known as **bass instruments** (their music usually uses the bass clef). A lot of instruments fit this pattern, but watch out for some that don't.

**4** Write a tune for cello using the notes of the tonic triad in F major to the given rhythm. Use a key signature and finish on the tonic.

**5** Look at the tunes you have written and add some musical words and symbols that you know. Also see page 51 for those for Grade 3.

# Anacrusis

**Anacrusis** is the word that describes the note or notes of a piece that a composer often writes before the first full bar. These are often called the **up-beat** (or **up-beats** if there is more than one note).

Here is an example of a song that starts with an anacrusis:

Traditional (German)

Look at the coloured boxes above. If you add together the first note (a quaver anacrusis) and the last note (a dotted crotchet) they make a full ²/₄ bar.

Notice that the first repeat mark in this piece is put after the anacrusis so that there are no spare beats left over.

**1** Write a **G** in the last bar to agree with the anacrusis.

Traditional (English)

**2** Write a **C** in the last bar to agree with the anacrusis.

Traditional (English)

**3** Write a **G** in the last bar to agree with the anacrusis.

Schubert

**4** Write a rest in the last bar to agree with the anacrusis.

Zelter

**5** Add up-bow signs above each anacrusis in tasks 1-3.

# Quaver triplets

Sometimes composers writing in simple time want to divide the beat into three equal parts. When the beat is a crotchet they write **quaver triplets** – three quavers to be played in the time of two. For example:

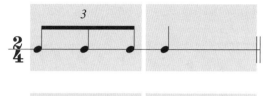

These rhythms (shown here in simple then compound time) sound the same even though they are written differently:

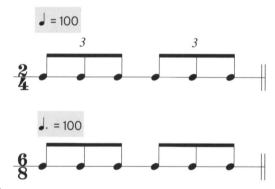

**1** Write some quaver triplets to agree with each time signature.

**2** Write the correct time signatures.

Chopin

Mozart

Beethoven

**3** Using quaver triplets, write a broken chord using the tonic triads of the following keys. Use patterns of three notes each time. Finish no more than two leger lines above or below the stave.

E minor going up

F major going down

A minor going up

G major going down

D minor going up

17

# Grouping quaver triplet rests

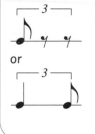
Sometimes composers want to use quaver rests within triplet groupings. **Brackets** are used to make the music easier to read.

Here are some possible groupings:

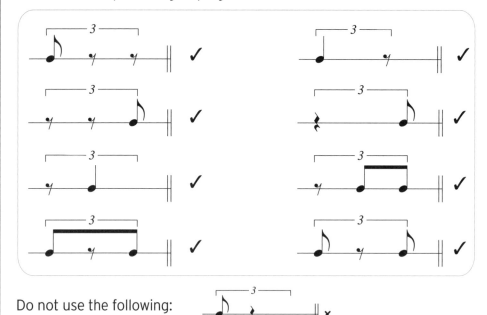

Do not use the following:

1  Add crotchet or quaver rests in the places marked by an asterisk (*) to complete the bars. Use brackets where necessary.

# The melodic minor scale

In Grade 2 you learned that natural and harmonic are two types of minor scale. There is another – the **melodic minor scale**.

The main characteristic of the melodic minor scale is that it sounds different going up from going down. It is often used in melodies where the composer wants to give the music a smooth shape, hence its name 'melodic'.

It differs from the natural minor scale only in that the 6th and 7th degrees are raised by a semitone going up. On the way down the 6th and 7th degrees are returned to natural minor scale pitch.

Here is a one-octave A melodic minor scale going up then down.

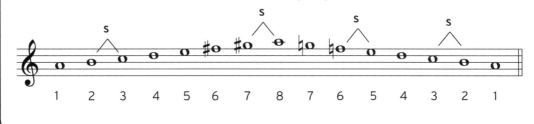

**1** Change the following scales from natural minor scales to melodic minor scales.

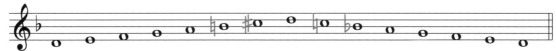

> **Handy tip!**
> Write in the degrees of the scale if you find it useful.

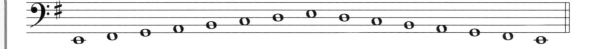

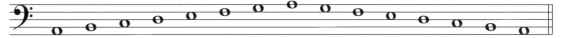

**2** Write a one-octave E melodic minor scale in minims going up then down. Use a key signature.

**3** Write a one-octave D melodic minor scale in minims going down then up. Use a key signature.

**4** Write a one-octave A melodic minor scale in crotchets going up then down. Use a key signature.

# The circle of 5ths

Here is the circle of 5ths that you will recognise from Grades 1 and 2. The highlighted keys are the only ones that you will need for Grade 3.

**Handy tip!**

This key is B flat major, not B major, because (as you learned in Grade 2) there is a perfect 5th between each key in the circle.

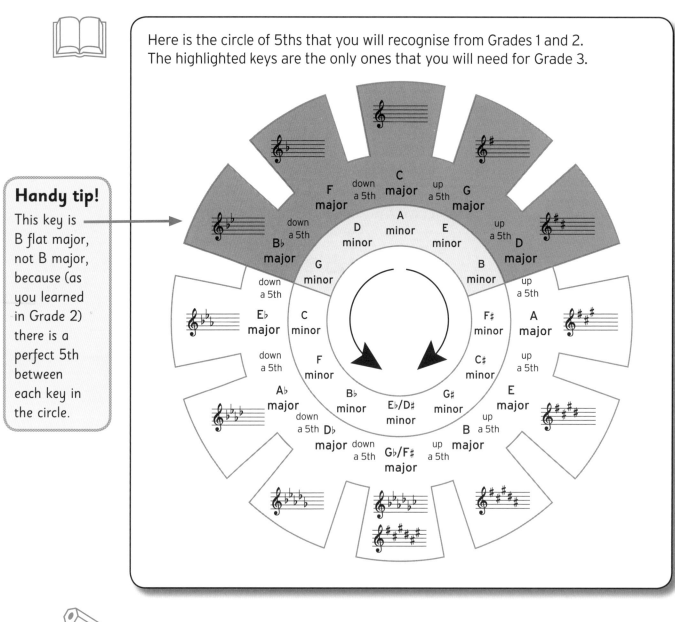

Using the circle of 5ths above, answer these questions:

**1** Which minor key has two flats in its key signature?  *G minor*

**2** Which major key has one flat in its key signature?_____

**3** Which minor key has two sharps in its key signature?_____

**4** Which major key has two sharps in its key signature?_____

**5** Which minor key has no flats or sharps in its key signature?_____

**6** Which minor key has one sharp in its key signature?_____

**7** Which minor key has one flat in its key signature?_____

# More about the new keys for Grade 3

The new keys for Grade 3 are **D major** and **B flat major** (and their relative minors **B** and **G**). They work like the others you have learned; the key signatures are there to make sure that the tone-semitone pattern is the same for each key.

**1** Write the key signature and the tonic triad in root position for each of the following keys.

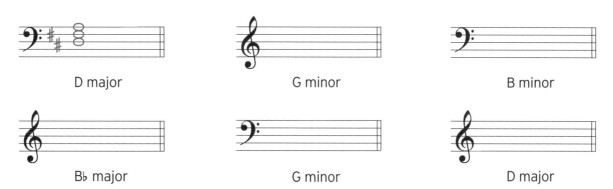

D major

G minor

B minor

B♭ major

G minor

D major

**2** Write a one-octave B flat major scale in minims going up then down. Use a key signature.

**3** Write a one-octave D major scale in minims going down then up. Use a key signature.

**4** Write a one-octave B flat major scale in crotchets going down then up. Do not use a key signature but write in the necessary accidentals.

**5** Write a one-octave G harmonic minor scale in minims going up then down. Use a key signature.

**6** Write a one-octave B natural minor scale in semibreves going down then up. Do not use a key signature but write in the necessary accidentals.

# Labelling scales

**1** Label these scales.

> **Remember**
> Melodic and natural minor scales sound the same going down, so either label is correct.

D melodic minor going up

**2** Label these scales. Here there are no key signatures so check the accidentals instead.

Bb major going down

# Second inversions of tonic triads

Until now you have written tonic triads in root position and first inversion. For Grade 3 you also need to be able to write tonic triads in **second inversion**.

Here is a tonic triad in C major in root position, then in first inversion:

If the first inversion triad is 'inverted' so that the fifth of the chord is at the bottom, the triad is in **second inversion**.

Here is a tonic triad in C major in second inversion:

**1** Write the key signature and the tonic triad in root and first inversions for each key shown. Then write its second inversion.

**Handy tip!**

Notice that the shape of each type of inversion looks similar, wherever it lies on the stave:

Root position

First inversion

Second inversion

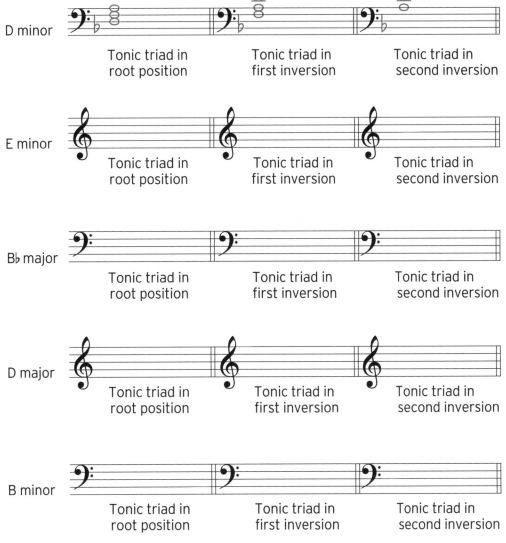

D minor — Tonic triad in root position / Tonic triad in first inversion / Tonic triad in second inversion

E minor — Tonic triad in root position / Tonic triad in first inversion / Tonic triad in second inversion

B♭ major — Tonic triad in root position / Tonic triad in first inversion / Tonic triad in second inversion

D major — Tonic triad in root position / Tonic triad in first inversion / Tonic triad in second inversion

B minor — Tonic triad in root position / Tonic triad in first inversion / Tonic triad in second inversion

**2** Label these tonic triads.

G major, second inversion

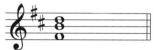

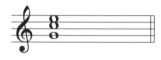

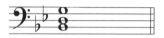

# Arpeggios

**Remember**

A one-octave arpeggio is made by 'breaking up' a tonic triad and playing each note separately with an extra tonic at the top.

As for Grade 1 and 2, the type of arpeggio that you need to know for Grade 3 is a one-octave arpeggio (shown here in the key of B minor).

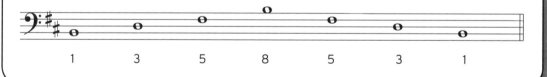

**1** Write the key signature for each key shown. Then write its one-octave arpeggio in the rhythm given below.

D major going up then down

G minor going down then up

B flat major going up then down

F major going down then up

**2** Label these one-octave arpeggios.

Bb major arpeggio going up then down

# Broken chords

**1** Using minims, write a broken chord using G minor tonic triad (going up). Use patterns of three notes each time. Finish on the first **G** above the stave.

> **Remember**
>
> A broken chord, like an arpeggio, is made by 'breaking up' a chord. Sometimes you can find one-octave arpeggios within larger broken chord patterns.

**2** Using quavers, write a broken chord using D minor tonic triad (going up). Use patterns of three notes each time. Finish on the first **D** above the stave.

**3** Using quavers, write a broken chord using G minor tonic triad (going up). Use patterns of four notes each time. Finish on the first **G** above the stave.

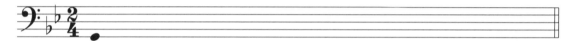

**4** Using triplet quavers, write a broken chord using B flat major tonic triad (going up). Use patterns of three notes each time. Finish on the first **B flat** above the stave.

**5** Using minims, write a broken chord using B minor tonic triad (going down). Use patterns of three notes each time. Finish on the first **B** below the stave.

**6** Using quavers, write a broken chord using D major tonic triad (going down). Use patterns of three notes each time. Finish on the **F sharp** in the first space.

**7** Using quavers, write a broken chord using E minor tonic triad (going down). Use patterns of three notes each time. Finish on the first **E** below the stave.

# Working out the key of a piece

For Grade 3 you need to be able to recognise more major and minor keys (see page 20).

Here are two examples to remind you how to work out the key each time.

**1**

Mozart

- Are there flats or sharps in the key signature and, if so, how many? *Yes, two sharps, so the key could be D major or B minor*

- Are there any accidentals in the music, that could be the raised 6th or 7th degrees in the relative minor? *No*

- Are there any other reasons to think that the key is D major? *Yes, the first few bars are based around the one-octave arpeggio of D*

   Answer: *The key is D major*

**2**

Mozart

**Remember**

The composer may be using the melodic minor scale to give the music a smooth shape (see page 19).

- Are there flats or sharps in the key signature and, if so, how many? *Yes, two flats, so the key could be B flat major or G minor*

- Are there any accidentals in the music that could be the raised 6th or 7th degrees in the relative minor? *Yes (so the key is probably a minor)*

- Are there any other reasons to think that the key is G minor? *Yes, much of the music is based around the tonic triad of G minor and the last note is G*

   Answer: *The key is G minor*
   *(It is not necessary to state 'melodic' or 'harmonic' when describing the key.)*

**1** Use the questions on the previous page to work out the keys.

Tchaikovsky

Key:_____

Johann Strauss II

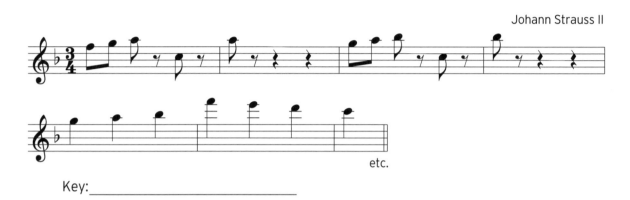

etc.

Key:_____

Mendelssohn

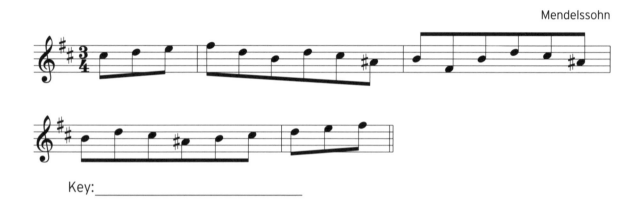

Key:_____

Corelli

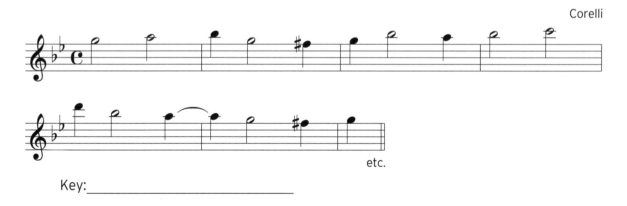

etc.

Key:_____

Mahler

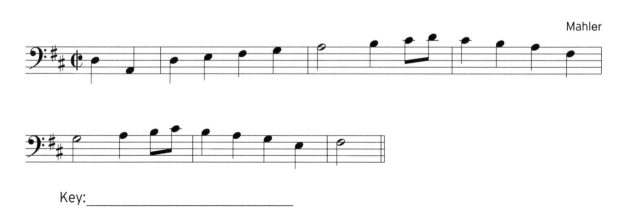

Key:_____

# Intervals – major and minor 6ths and 7ths

In Grade 2 you learned how to tell the difference between major and minor 2nds and 3rds. For Grade 3 you also need to know the difference between **major** and **minor 6ths** and **7ths**.

**Remember**

First, count up from the bottom note to get the interval number.

Major and minor 6ths

Interval: Major 6th

In major keys there is always an interval of a **major 6th** between the 1st and 6th degrees of the scale.

Interval: Minor 6th

In natural minor scales there is always an interval of a **minor 6th** between the 1st and 6th degrees of the scale.

**Handy tip!**

Play and listen to these intervals so that you learn how they sound.

Major and minor 7ths

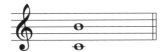

Interval: Major 7th

In major keys there is always an interval of a **major 7th** between the 1st and 7th degrees of the scale.

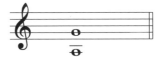

Interval: Minor 7th

In natural minor scales there is always an interval of a **minor 7th** between the 1st and 7th degrees of the scale.

**1** Name the following intervals.

Interval: Minor 6th

Interval: _____

Interval: _____

Interval: _____

Interval: _____

Interval: _____

Interval: _____

Interval: _____

Interval: _____

**2** Name the following Grade 3 intervals.

Interval: _Major 7th_

Interval: _____

Interval: _____

Interval: _____

Interval: _____

Interval: _____

Interval: _____

Interval: _____

Interval: _____

Interval: _____

Interval: _____

Interval: _____

Interval: _____

Interval: _____

Interval: _____

**Remember**

Where there is a key signature it might affect the interval.

Interval: _____

Interval: _____

Interval: _____

Interval: _____

Interval: _____

Interval: _____

Interval: _____

Interval: _____

Interval: _____

# Real and tonal sequences

For Grade 3 you need to know that some sequences are **real** (all the intervals within the sequence are the same in each tune pattern), like this:

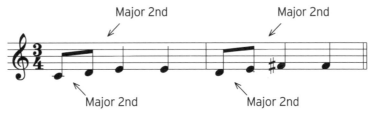

Others are **tonal** (the shape of the tune pattern is the same but the intervals within the sequence are different), like this:

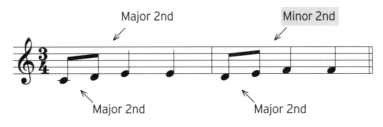

In a long sequence there may be a mixture of real and tonal sequences.

**1** Write a bracket (⌐¬ or ⌐¬) to show the sequence. Then label it real or tonal.

Beethoven

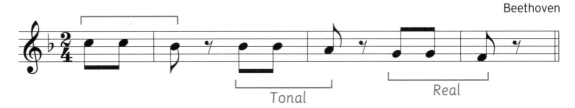

Traditional (Welsh)

Beethoven

Traditional (English)

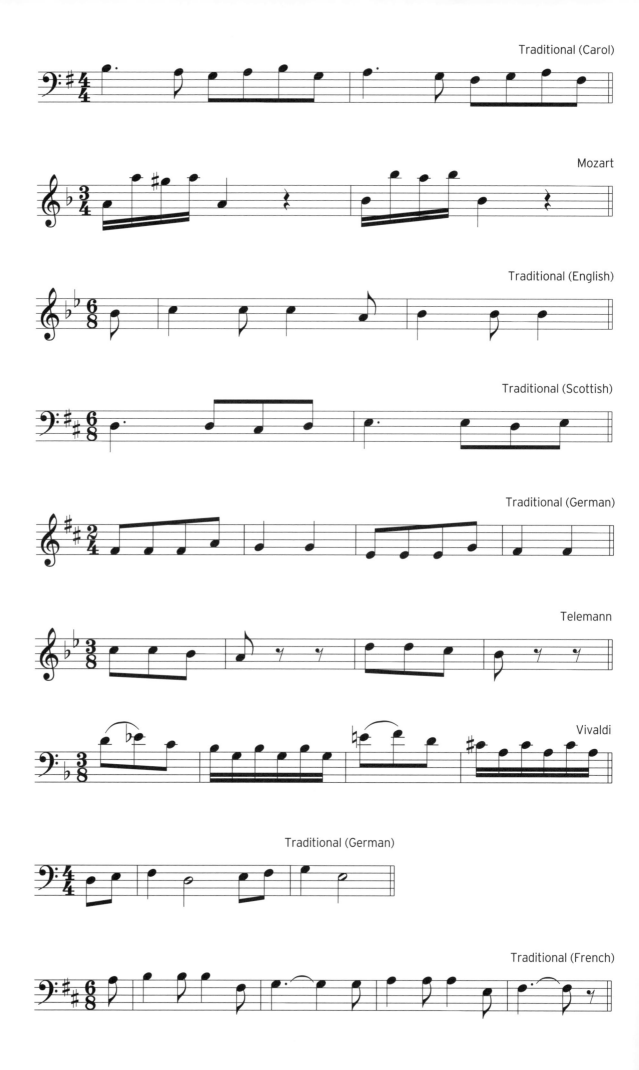

# Dominant triads in major keys

As you know, the 1st degree of the scale and its triad are very important to the sound of any key. The 5th degree (the **dominant**) – and the triad built on it – is also significant within a key. The dominant of the scale can also be called **soh**.

Here is the scale of C major with triads built on the 1st and 5th degrees:

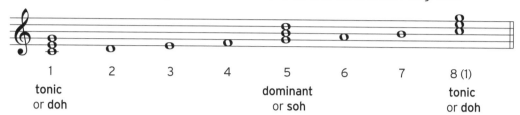

| 1 | 2 | 3 | 4 | 5 | 6 | 7 | 8 (1) |
|---|---|---|---|---|---|---|---|
| tonic<br>or **doh** | | | | dominant<br>or **soh** | | | tonic<br>or **doh** |

Here is the dominant triad in the key of C major:

### Remember

The triad on the 8th degree of the scale is always labelled chord I (or i) and not chord VIII (or viii).

The dominant triad is often labelled with a Roman numeral – V, showing that the chord is built on the 5th degree of the scale. In the key of C major, for example:

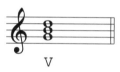

V

Composers could also label the dominant triad in C major like this, especially if they are writing for guitar. In fact any chord that uses just the notes **G**, **B** and **D** (whatever the register) can have this label:

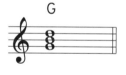

G

**1** Here are some major scales. Write triads on the tonic and dominant degrees of the scales and label them with Roman numerals.

### Remember

Write Roman numerals below the stave(s).

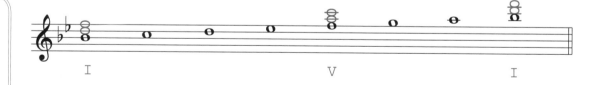

I                    V                    I

**Remember**

Write chord symbols above the stave(s).

**2** Here are some major scales. Write triads on the tonic and dominant degrees of the scales and label them with chord symbols.

B♭                                              F                                              B♭

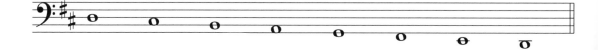

# Dominant triads in minor keys

Dominant triads in minor keys are built on the 5th degree of the minor scale.

Here is the harmonic minor scale of A minor with triads built on the 1st and 5th degrees:

| 1 | 2 | 3 | 4 | 5 | 6 | 7 | 8 (1) |
|---|---|---|---|---|---|---|---|
| tonic | | | | dominant | | | tonic |

Here is the dominant triad in the key of A minor. The **G** is raised because **G sharp** is the 7th degree of the A harmonic minor scale; this is the scale to use when you think about chords in Grade 3.

The dominant triad is often labelled with a Roman numeral (V) – showing that the chord is built on the 5th degree of the scale. Composers could also label the dominant triad in A minor using chord symbols like this:

In fact any chord that uses just the notes **E**, **G sharp** and **B** (whatever the register) can have this label.

**1** Here are some harmonic minor scales. Write triads on the 1st and 5th degrees of the scales and label them with Roman numerals.

**2** Here are some harmonic minor scales. Write triads on the 1st and 5th degrees of the scales and label them with chord symbols.

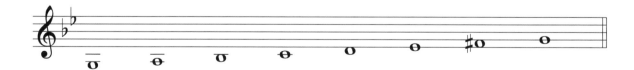

# Chord progression

Chord progression means the order in which chords move from one to another in a piece of music.

**1** Label the triads with Roman numerals to show the chord progression.

(B minor)   i            V            V            i

(E minor)

(C major)

(G minor)

**2** Label the triads with chord symbols to show the chord progression.

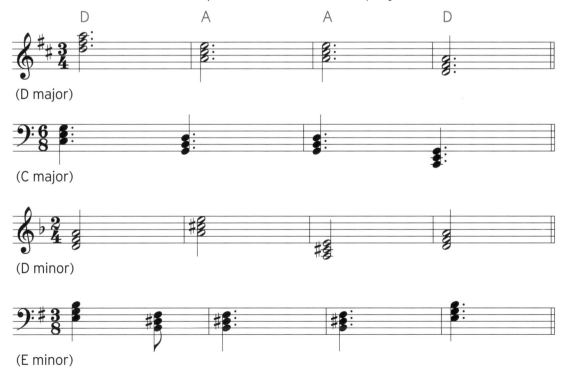

D            A            A            D

(D major)

(C major)

(D minor)

(E minor)

# Similar motion

Music moves in **similar motion** if two parts (or more) move in parallel or in the same direction. Keyboard players often play scales in similar motion. Here is a C major scale in similar motion an octave apart:

Tunes moving in similar motion are rather like parallel lines – the parts could go on forever and never meet.

**1** Write two more repeats of these bars to make ostinati that move in similar motion.

# Contrary motion

Music moves in **contrary motion** if two parts (or more) move away from one another or towards one another. Keyboard players often play scales in contrary motion. Here is a C major scale in contrary motion:

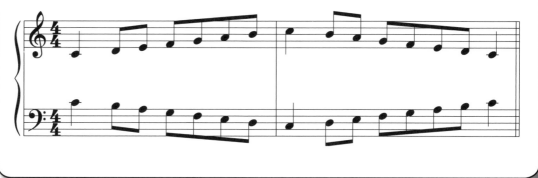

**1** Write two more repeats of these bars to make ostinati that move in contrary motion.

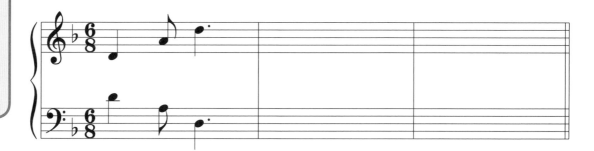

# Writing a bass line

## In major keys

**1** Use the root of each triad shown by the Roman numerals to write a bass line.

(G major)  I      V      V      I

(D major)  I      I      V      I

(B♭ major)  I      I      V      I

(F major)  I      I      V      I

**2** Use the root of each triad shown by the chord symbols to write a bass line.

C      G      G      C

**Did you know?**

The **bass line** is the line of music that is usually at the lowest register in a piece of music.

**Handy tip!**

A strong bass line often moves in contrary motion to the tune. Do not let the bass line move in similar motion in perfect 5ths or octaves with the tune; this sounds weak and will lose you marks in your exam.

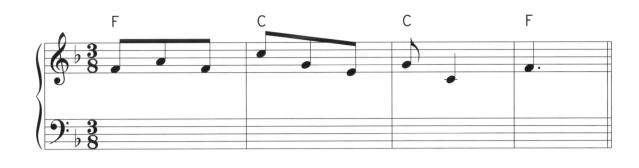

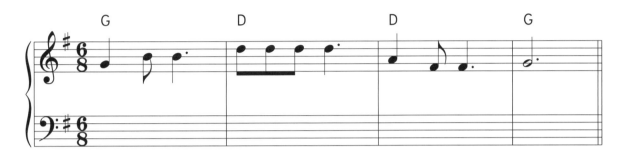

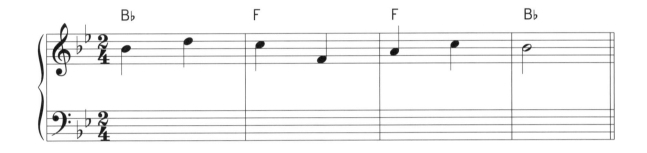

## In minor keys

**1** Use the root of each triad shown by the Roman numerals to write a bass line.

(B minor)  i          i          V          i

(A minor)  i          V          V          i

(E minor)    i            i            V            i

(D minor)    i            V            V            i

**2** Use the root of each triad shown by the chord symbols to write a bass line.

Em           Em           B            Em

Am           Am           E            Am

Gm           D            D            Gm

Bm           Bm           F#           Bm

# Writing a tune

## In major keys

**1** Use notes from the tonic or dominant triads shown by the Roman numerals to write a tune above the bass line.

**Did you know?**

A strong tune often moves in contrary motion to the bass line. Do not let the tune move in similar motion in perfect 5ths or octaves with the bass line; this sounds weak and will lose you marks in your exam.

(B♭ major)  I  I  V  I

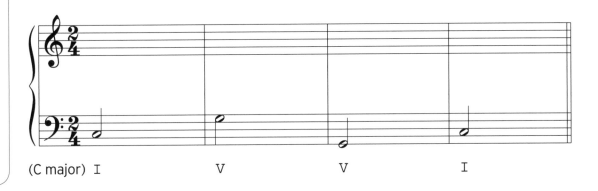

(C major)  I  V  V  I

**Handy tip!**

Try to hear in your head the tunes that you write. Play or sing them too so that you really know how they sound.

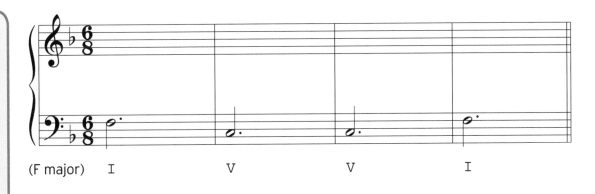

(F major)  I  V  V  I

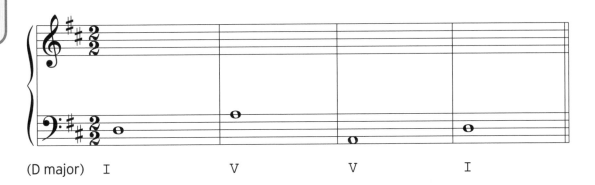

(D major)  I  V  V  I

**2** Use notes from the tonic or dominant triads shown by the chord symbols to write a tune above the bass line.

## In minor keys

**1** Use notes from the tonic or dominant triads shown by the Roman numerals to write a tune above the bass line.

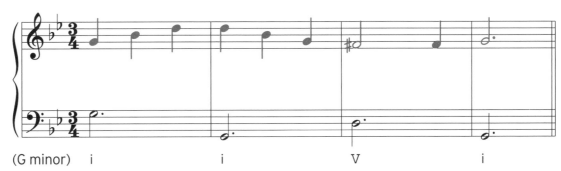

(G minor)    i                       i                  V                i

**Remember**

Remember to raise the 7th degree when you use the dominant triad because the large Roman numeral shows you that there is a major 3rd at the bottom of the triad.

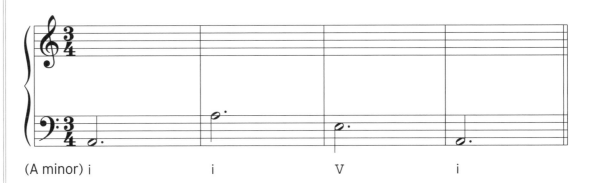

(A minor) i                     i                V               i

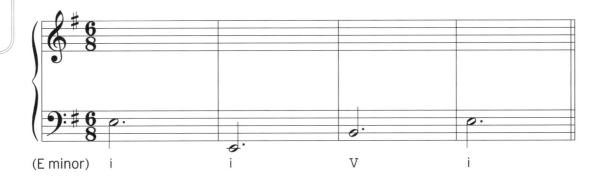

(E minor)    i                   i                V               i

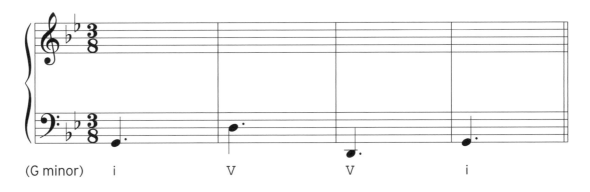

(G minor)   i                 V               V               i

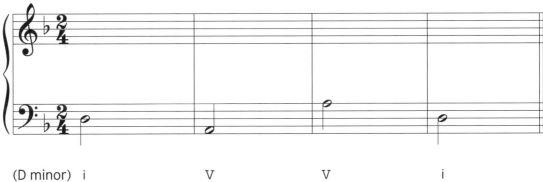

(D minor)  i                 V               V               i

**2** Use notes from the tonic or dominant triads shown by the chord symbols to write a tune above the bass line.

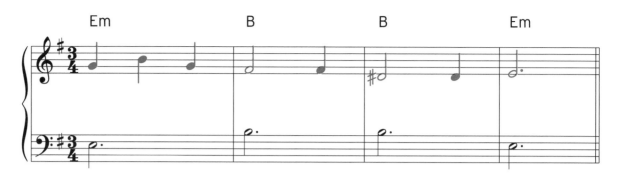

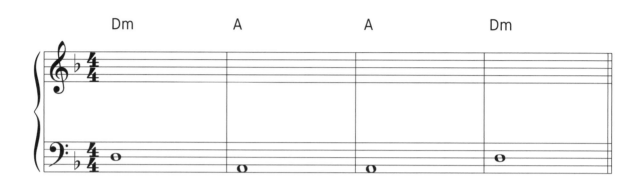

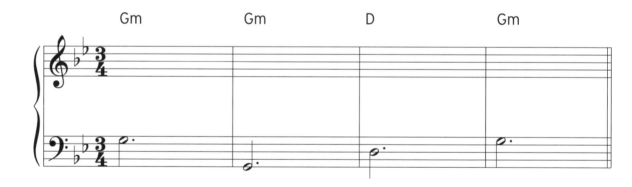

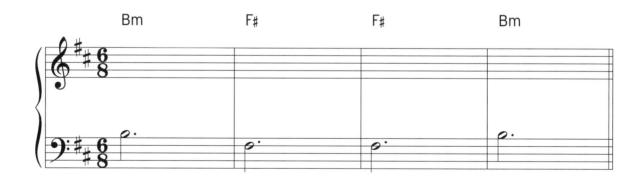

**3** Look at the tunes you have written and add some musical words and symbols that you know. Also see page 51 for those for Grade 3.

# 4-part chords

### Did you know?

4-part choirs usually have parts for **soprano**, **alto**, **tenor** and **bass** voices. The soprano and alto parts are often written on one stave (with a treble clef) and the tenor and bass parts on another stave (with a bass clef). So that the parts are not confused, the stems go up for soprano and tenor and down for alto and bass.

See page 63 for the commonly used ranges of soprano, alto, tenor and bass voices.

Music written for 4-part choir often uses chords that contain the three notes of the triad (whatever the register) and an extra root, making a total of four parts.

Using two roots in a chord means that the sound of the root stands out as being the most prominent part of the chord.

Here is an example of the way a tonic chord in the key of A minor might be written for SATB (soprano, alto, tenor and bass voices).

You will see that there are two **A**s (the root of the triad) in the bass; also, that the notes of the chord are spread out fairly evenly across the staves. This makes the chord sound clear and balanced and gives all the singers a note to sing which suits their range. In general, notes can be put closer together in the treble than in the bass, where they will sound indistinct if they are not well spaced out.

**1** Circle the two roots in the following chords.

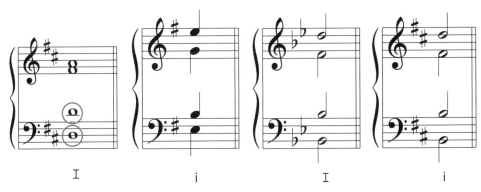

### Handy tip!

Play the tonic triad in the key of C major high and low on a keyboard to understand the difference that register can make to the sound of a chord.

**2** Using minims, write out 4-part chords for SATB using the chords shown by the Roman numerals. Double the root in each case and make sure that each chord is in root position.

### Did you know?

There is more than one way of writing a well-balanced chord.

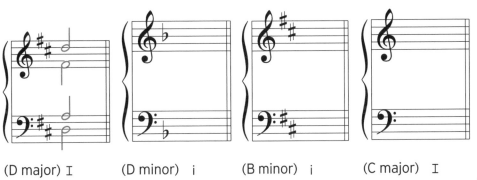

(D major) I     (D minor) i     (B minor) i     (C major) I

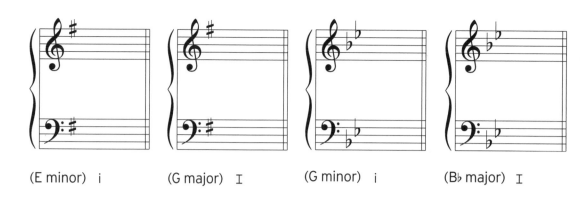

(E minor) i      (G major) I      (G minor) i      (B♭ major) I

# Perfect cadences

Cadences are like punctuation in sentences. They give structure and meaning to the music. A **perfect cadence** acts as a musical full stop and is made by following the dominant chord with the tonic (V-I, or V-i). For Grade 3 you need to be able to recognise this chord progression in a piece of music.

**Did you know?**

The 7th degree usually leads up to the tonic when it is part of the dominant chord in the last cadence of a piece. That is why it is called the **leading note**.

Here is a perfect cadence in C major:

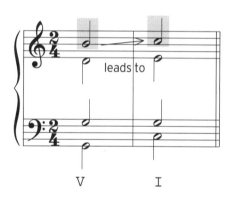

A perfect cadence could look like this too:

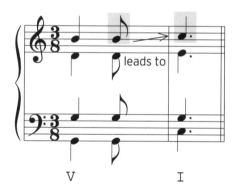

Here is a perfect cadence in A minor:

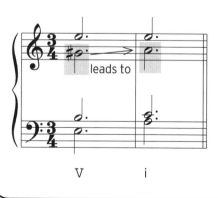

**Handy tip!**

Play these cadences (or ask your teacher if you need help).

# Transposing tunes up or down an octave

If a piece of music is written too high or low for an instrument to play – or for a voice to sing – it is sometimes necessary to move it to a more comfortable register. Look at this:

Traditional (Spiritual)

This is easy to play on a treble instrument (for example, the violin or flute) but difficult to play on a bass instrument (such as cello or bassoon). Transposing it down an octave into the bass clef makes it easy for bass instruments to play:

You can also do the opposite to transpose a tune up an octave from the bass clef for a treble instrument to play.

Use the following method:

- Write the new clef and adjust the position of the key signature
- Look at the first note of the tune and find the equivalent note (up or down an octave)
- Write this note in the new clef, checking that you are in the correct register using **Middle C** as a reference point
- Check this is correct
- Write out the tune with the same intervals between the notes and write in any accidentals
- Check that the last note that you write has the same letter name as the last note of the original tune

**Handy tip!**

See page 62 for the ranges of violin, cello, flute and bassoon.

**1** Transpose the following tunes down an octave into the bass clef to make them suitable for a cello or bassoon to play.

Mozart

Traditional (Czech)

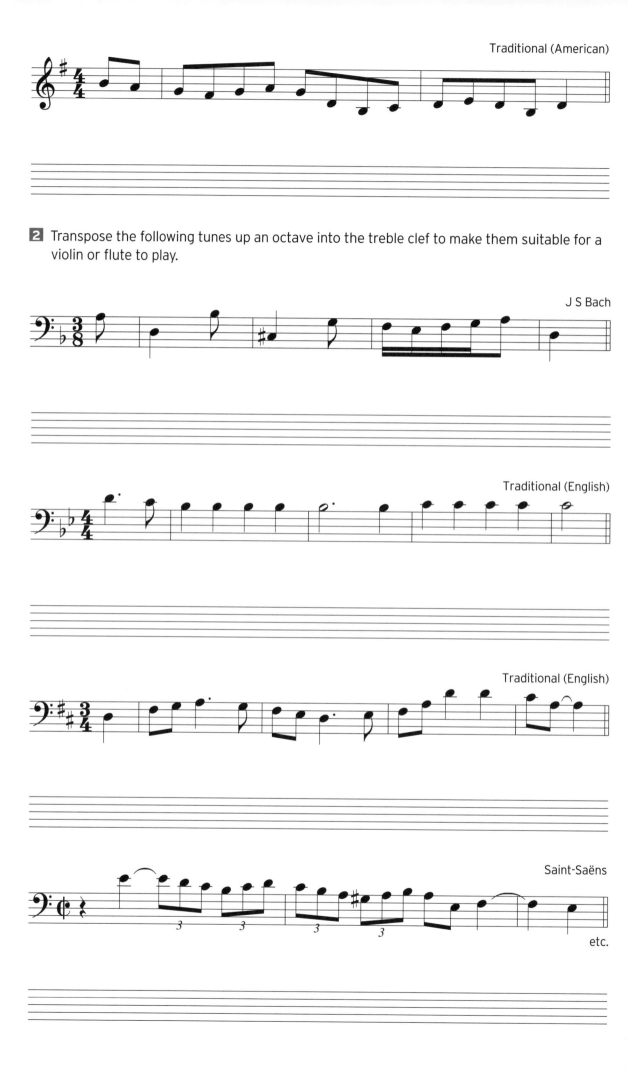

Traditional (American)

**2** Transpose the following tunes up an octave into the treble clef to make them suitable for a violin or flute to play.

J S Bach

Traditional (English)

Traditional (English)

Saint-Saëns

etc.

# Musical words and symbols

A written piece of music can contain lots of information – not just the notes to be played and in what rhythm, but **how** to play it. For Grade 3 you need to know the following, in addition to the Grade 1 and 2 words and symbols:

## Articulation marks
(tell a player how to play the notes, e.g. smoothly or with an accent)

*marcato* (*marc.*) – marked, accented

or   *semi-staccato* – half-staccato, halfway between legato and staccato

## Expression marks
(tell a player what kind of feeling/mood to give the music)

*dolce* – sweetly

*leggiero* – lightly

*marziale* – march-like

*tranquillo* – calmly

*vivo* – lively

## Instrument-specific instructions

⊓ – to be played with a down-bow (bowed string instruments)

∨ – to be played with an up-bow (bowed string instruments)

## Tempo marks and other signs
(tell a player what speed to play the music and other details)

*al, alla* – like

*a tempo* – in time *or* at the speed that the piece started

*con* – with

*da capo al Fine* – go back to the beginning and play until it says *Fine*
               (*Fine* means 'the end')

*e, ed* – and

*ma* – but

*meno* – less

*mosso, moto* – movement

*non* – not

*poco* – little

*più* – more

# Analysis

**1** Look at the following piece and answer the questions on the opposite page.

## In the Woods and Meadows

Traditional (German)

1. In which key is this piece? __B flat major__

2. What note is the tonic in this piece? __B flat__

3. What note is soh in this piece? __F__

4. Write a Roman numeral below the last chord of this piece to show that the tonic chord accompanies the tune here.

5. Write a Roman numeral below the last dotted crotchet beat of bar 23 to show that the dominant chord accompanies the tune here.

6. Looking at the chord progression you have written by doing questions 4 and 5, name the cadence that ends this piece.

    __Perfect cadence__

7. Circle a one-octave arpeggio in this piece.

8. How many notes higher or lower is the sequence in bars 9-12 repeated (treble part)?

    __The sequences repeat one note higher__

9. Is the sequence in bars 9-12 real or tonal (treble part)? __It is tonal__

10. Why are the quavers beamed together in 3s in bar 19 (bass part)?

    __Because the main beat is a dotted crotchet__

11. Does this piece start on an up-beat or a down-beat? __An up-beat__

12. What is the musical word for music that does not start on the first beat of the bar?

    __Anacrusis__

13. How many quavers could fit into the tied **B flat** in bar 8 (treble part)? __4 quavers__

14. Look at the boxed notes in bars 20-22. Comment on the pitch.

    __The notes in the bass part are one octave lower than those in the treble__

15. What does **Vivo** mean? __Lively__

**2** Look at the following piece and answer the questions on the opposite page.

## The Bagpipers

Goedicke

1. In which key is this piece?_____

2. What note is the tonic in this piece?_____

3. What note is the dominant in this piece?_____

4. Write a chord symbol above all the bars where the music has a chord built on the tonic in the bass line to show that the tonic chord accompanies the tune here.

5. On which degree of the scale does the music arrive in bar 8 (𝅗𝅥.)?_____

6. Look at the boxed notes in bars 8 and 9. Comment on the pitch.

   _____

7. Look at beats 2 and 3 in bar 11. Does the music move in similar or contrary motion?

   _____

8. Name the interval between the two notes marked with asterisks (*) in bar 14.

   _____

9. Why are there only three beats in bar 20 even though the time signature for the piece is common time?

   _____

10. Look at bars 1-4 (treble part). In which bars is there an exact repeat of this music later in the piece?

   _____

11. Write the sign for *marcato* that the composer uses in this piece and explain what it means.

   _____

12. Name the pitch of the last note of the piece (treble part)._____

13. What does **Allegretto** mean?_____

14. In which bar should the player begin to slow down a little?

   _____

15. What does *a tempo* in bar 12 mean?_____

**3** Look at the following piece and answer the questions on the opposite page.

## The Miller of Dee

Traditional (English) arr. Hand

1. In which key is this piece? _____

2. What note is the leading note in this piece?_____

3. Write a chord symbol above the last chord of this piece to show that the tonic chord accompanies the tune here.

4. Write a chord symbol above the last dotted crochet beat in bar 15 to show that the dominant chord accompanies the tune here.

5. Looking at the chord progression you have written by doing questions 3 and 4, name the type of cadence that ends this piece.

   _____

6. How many notes higher or lower is the sequence in bars 9-10 repeated (treble part)?

   _____

7. Is the sequence in bars 9 and 10 real or tonal (treble part)?

   _____

8. Name the interval between the two notes marked with asterisks (*) in bars 5-6.

   _____

9. How many phrases make up this piece?_____

10. Why do the phrases begin on the last quaver of the bar?_____

11. Which phrases end with a V-i chord progression?_____

12. Which phrase ends on the dominant chord?_____

13. What does *cresc.* mean?_____

14. Is this piece in simple or compound time?_____

15. What does *leggiero* mean?_____

# Sample examination paper

---

## Section 1 (10 marks)

*Put a tick (✓) in the box next to the correct answer.*

### Example

Name this note:

A ☐   D ☐   C ☑

This shows that you think **C** is the correct answer.

---

1.1   Name the circled note:

D ☐   F♮ ☐   F♯ ☐

1.2   Add the total number of minim beats in these tied notes.

4 ☐   4½ ☐   5 ☐

1.3   Which sign shows a semiquaver rest?

𝄾· ☐   𝄿 ☐   𝄾 ☐

1.4   Which is the correct time signature?

$\frac{3}{2}$ ☐   $\frac{12}{8}$ ☐   $\frac{9}{8}$ ☐

1.5   The minor key with two sharps in its key signature is:

D minor ☐   B minor ☐   E minor ☐

1.6   Which note is the tonic of the minor key shown by this key signature?

B♭ ☐   G ☐   F ☐

---

Trinity College London reserves the right to alter the format and content of examination papers at any time. Please ensure that you consult the latest syllabus and our website – www.trinitycollege.co.uk – before entering for an examination.

*Put a tick (✓) in the box next to the correct answer.*

1.7    Which chord symbol fits above this dominant triad?

Em ☐    B ☐    Bm ☐

☐

1.8    Name this interval:

Major 6th ☐    Minor 7th ☐    Major 7th ☐

☐

1.9    Name this triad:

Tonic triad of A minor in first inversion ☐
Tonic triad of A minor in root position ☐
Tonic triad of C major in root position ☐

☐

1.10    What does *meno* mean?

like ☐    more ☐    less ☐

☐

# Section 2 (15 marks)

2.1    Write a one-octave B♭ major scale in crotchets going down then up. Do not use a key signature but write in the necessary accidentals.

☐

2.2    Write the key signature for the key shown. Then write its one-octave arpeggio in the rhythm given below.

B minor going up then down

☐

# Section 3 (10 marks)

3.1    Circle five different mistakes in the following music, then write it out correctly.

*p*

**Vivace**

☐

## Section 4 (15 marks)

4.1 Transpose this tune down an octave into the bass clef to make it suitable for a cello or bassoon to play.

Anon.

## Section 5 (15 marks)

5.1 Using minims, write out 4-part chords for SATB using the chords shown by the Roman numerals. Double the root in each case and make sure that each chord is in root position.

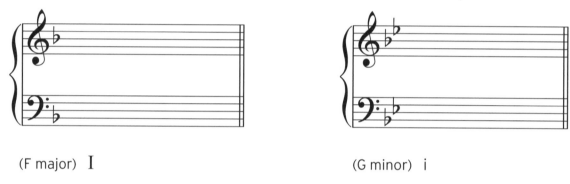

(F major) I

(G minor) i

## Section 6 (15 marks)

6.1 Use notes from the tonic or dominant triads shown by the chord symbols to write a tune above the bass line.

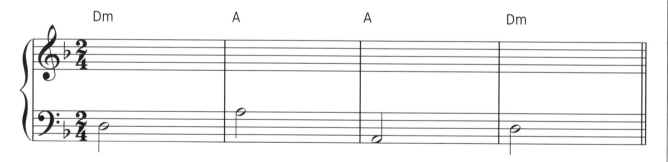

Dm          A          A          Dm

# Section 7 (20 marks)

Look at the following piece and answer the questions below.

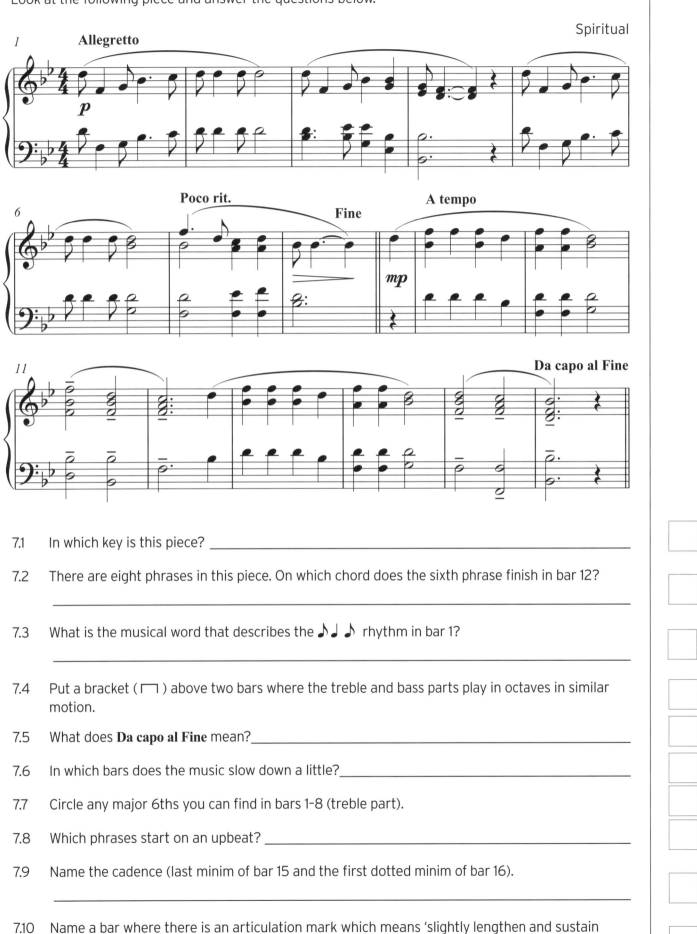

Spiritual

7.1    In which key is this piece? _____

7.2    There are eight phrases in this piece. On which chord does the sixth phrase finish in bar 12?

_____

7.3    What is the musical word that describes the ♪ ♩ ♪ rhythm in bar 1?

_____

7.4    Put a bracket ( ⌐¬ ) above two bars where the treble and bass parts play in octaves in similar motion.

7.5    What does **Da capo al Fine** mean?_____

7.6    In which bars does the music slow down a little?_____

7.7    Circle any major 6ths you can find in bars 1-8 (treble part).

7.8    Which phrases start on an upbeat? _____

7.9    Name the cadence (last minim of bar 15 and the first dotted minim of bar 16).

_____

7.10    Name a bar where there is an articulation mark which means 'slightly lengthen and sustain the note'._____

**Remember**

If the notes of a tune fit into an instrument or voice range then it is suitable for that instrument or voice to play or sing.

## Instrument ranges

The ranges given here are for players of approximately Grade 5 standard. The complete ranges (especially for string instruments) go much higher.

**String instruments**

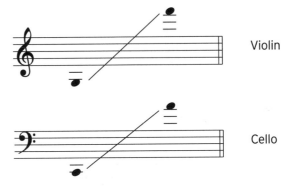

Violin

Cello

**Woodwind instruments**

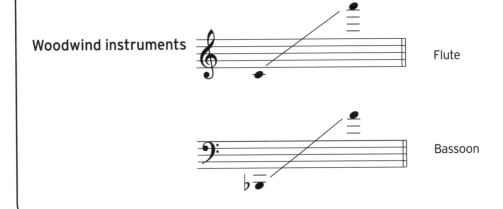

Flute

Bassoon